SAMMY
SOSA

SAMMY
SOSA

GABRIEL FLYNN
THE CHILD'S WORLD®, INC.

ON THE COVER...

Front cover: Sammy gets ready to throw the ball during batting practice in San Diego on September 15, 1998.
Page 2: Sammy signals to the crowd during a 1999 game.

Library of Congress Cataloging-in-Publication Data
Flynn, Gabriel.
Sammy Sosa / by Gabriel Flynn.
p. cm.
Includes index.
ISBN 1-56766-832-1 (lib. reinforced. : alk. paper)
1. Sosa, Sammy, 1968——Juvenile literature.
2. Baseball players—Dominican Republic—Biography—Juvenile literature.
[1. Sosa, Sammy, 1968- 2. Baseball players.] I. Title.
GV865.S59 F59 2000
796.357'092—dc21
00-029038

PHOTO CREDITS

© AP/Wide World Photos: cover, 6, 9, 10, 13, 15, 16, 19, 20, 22
© Rob Tringali, Jr./SportsChrome-USA: 2

TABLE OF CONTENTS

HIS HOMELAND

About 750 miles southeast of Florida lies a small nation called the Dominican Republic. This Spanish-speaking island lies between Haiti and Puerto Rico. More than 7 million people live there. It is a poor country. The favorite sport of the people who live there is baseball.

Many famous baseball players have come from the Dominican Republic, including Pedro Martinez, George Bell, and Juan Marichal. But the most famous Dominican player is Sammy Sosa.

Sammy is from the town of San Pedro de Macoris. This is a poor fishing town of 80,000 people on the southeastern coast of the island. Most children here play baseball at a very young age. But Sammy didn't even start playing baseball until age 14. He was too busy working odd jobs such as shining shoes, washing cars, cleaning yards, and selling fruit. Why did he work so hard? Since his father had died, he had to earn money for his family.

 Sammy watches the ball go out of the park during the All-Star Game home run derby on July 10, 1995.

ELEMENTARY SCHOOL
2315 HIGH MEADOW ROAD
NAPERVILLE, IL 60564

HIS DREAM

Like many young players, Sammy had a dream. His dream was to come to America to play professional baseball. When he was 16 years old, he came to the United States, but he wasn't **drafted** by any team. The Texas Rangers finally signed him to a **contract.** He started in the **minor leagues.** He played hard and had to work his way up until he finally made the **major leagues.** He played his first game for the Texas Rangers on June 16, 1989. He was just 20 years old. He played against the New York Yankees and got two hits. Five days later he hit his first home run, against Roger Clemens of the Boston Red Sox.

After only a month he was traded to the Chicago White Sox. He played fairly well for the next few years. On March 30, 1992, he was traded to the Chicago Cubs. He didn't play very much at first because he hurt his hand and broke his ankle. Would he ever become the great player he knew he could be? Sammy set out to prove he could.

Sammy jokes around in the dugout on his first day as a Chicago Cub.

BECOMING AN ALL-STAR

In 1993, Sammy played very well. He hit 33 home runs and stole 36 bases. He became the first Cubs player ever to reach 30 home runs and 30 stolen bases in one season. In 1994, he again played well. He continued to hit home runs and showed how powerful he was. Sammy hit one ball so hard, it went 461 feet—traveling over the 30-foot-high fence in Colorado's Mile High Stadium. He was the first player ever to clear this fence.

Sammy began to play with pride. He wore number 21 on his uniform in honor of Roberto Clemente, who is in the **Hall of Fame.** Whenever he got a hit he would touch his heart and raise up two fingers in a V as a sign to his mother and his family back home. It was also a sign for his fans both in America and in the Dominican Republic.

In 1995, Sammy was finally recognized as one of the league's best players. He led his team with 36 homers, the second-best total in the entire league. He also had 34 steals, and was chosen to play in the All-Star game. In 1996, he amazed his fans by hitting two home runs in the same **inning.** No Cubs player had ever done that before. He hit 40 homers that year to lead his team. He was showing that he was a great player.

Sammy jogs toward third base after hitting a two-run homer against the Florida Marlins on June 21, 1994.

THE HOME RUN RACE

At the beginning of the 1998 season, Sammy didn't play very well. On May 25, almost two months into the season, he had hit only nine home runs. That would be doing well for many players, but not for Sammy. Mark McGwire of the St. Louis Cardinals already had 24 homers by this time. Many people began to talk about how well Mark was playing. Many wondered if he could break the all-time home run record. This record was held by Roger Maris, who hit 61 home runs for the New York Yankees in 1961. Maris broke Babe Ruth's legendary record of 60 homers, set in 1927. It was considered the most famous record in all of sports.

ON A RECORD PACE

But did Sammy's slow start discourage him? No! With all the attention focused on Mark, Sammy was able to play without any pressure. Over the next 30 days he belted 21 homers—the most home runs ever hit in that short a time. On June 1, he slammed two homers against the Florida Marlins. By the end of June he had hit 20, which was the most ever in one month. By midseason, when he was chosen to play in his second All-Star game, he shared the spotlight with Mark. But could he or Mark break Maris's record? Only time would tell if the record would fall.

Sammy hits his 48th home run of the season against the St. Louis Cardinals on August 19, 1998.

Throughout the rest of the season, the two sluggers battled each other for the home run lead. On August 19, the Cardinals played the Cubs in Chicago's Wrigley Field. The stadium was sold out. Sammy and Mark were tied with 47 homers apiece. Sosa hit his 48th homer early in the game. But Mark hit two, including the one that won the game in the 10th inning.

During the rest of August and September, the home run lead went back and forth. Mark hit his 61st homer on September 7 and then broke the record the next night. Would Sammy be able to reach Maris's total, too? The baseball world would find out in six days.

THAT GREAT DAY

On September 13, the Cubs played the Milwaukee Brewers. In the fifth inning, pitcher Bronswell Patrick was ahead of Sammy, no balls and one strike. Sammy took a deep breath and hit the next pitch so hard that it soared 480 feet, over the left-field stands, and landed in the street. It was his 61st home run, tying Maris's total. The crowd jumped, cheered, and stomped its feet. Outside the stadium, fans chased Sammy's bouncing ball. After he rounded the bases, he got a long bear-hug from teammate Mark Grace. He went to the dugout and embraced the rest of his teammates.

Sammy leaps into the air as he watches his 62nd home run of the season leave the stadium on September 13, 1998.

Sammy saluted the TV camera by touching his heart and making his V sign. He then blew kisses and said, "I love you, mama." The crowd cheered louder and louder. He came out of the dugout, tipped his batting helmet, and waved to all the fans.

But Sammy wasn't finished. In the ninth inning he came up to bat for the last time. Eric Plunk threw him a pitch and. . .whack! He crushed the ball out of the stadium and into the street again! It was his 62nd homer, and he passed Maris's total! The game stopped as the crowd stood and shouted, "Sam-mee! Sam-mee!" for six minutes straight. The whole event was shown live on TV back in the Dominican Republic. And most important to Sammy, his mother saw it all!

REMEMBERING HIS PAST

Yes, Sammy is watched closely in his homeland. He has never forgotten the poverty that he experienced and that his country still endures. When his country was devastated by Hurricane Georges, he donated money to help the people rebuild. Because his country's schools are poor, he bought 250 computers for them. Elsa Wehr, principal of a San Pedro de Macoris public school, stated, "I don't remember any ball-player before [who has done] anything like that."

Sammy makes his V sign to a camera as he steps into the dugout after hitting his 62nd home run of the season.

But Sammy's kindness didn't stop there. He helped pay for a new ambulance for his hometown fire department. And what about children who want to learn to play baseball? He has paid for a baseball **academy** that provides rooms, food, and equipment for kids in his hometown who otherwise wouldn't have the chance to learn.

Sammy feels it is right to share his wealth with his home country. "That's what Sammy is," said Omar Minaya, one of the men who signed Sammy to his first contract when he was just 16. "The hope he has given to so many people, so many people from all parts of the world that may come from **third-world** nations like Sammy has."

THE MOST VALUABLE PLAYER

Sammy finished the season with 66 home runs. Although Mark McGwire hit 70, it was Sammy who was voted the National League's Most Valuable Player. Sammy finished the year first in runs batted in (RBIs) with 158, first in total bases with 416, and first in runs scored with 134. Cubs manager Jim Riggleman said, "You can't hardly put it into words. It's just been so unbelievable what he's done. . . . He's been huge for the city, for the [Cubs, and] for his teammates. It's just been an unbelievable story, the '98 season, with Sammy Sosa leading the way."

Sammy signs autographs for fans before a game against the San Diego Padres on September 14, 1998.

CONTINUING TO BE AN ALL-STAR

In 1999, Sammy continued his hot hitting. When it came time for the All-Star Game, he got the most votes of any National League player. It was his third All-Star Game. He played well all year, and by the time September came around, he was about to break another record. He had 59 home runs, and no player ever had hit more than 60 home runs two years in a row. Could Sammy be the first?

On September 18th, the Cubs played the Milwaukee Brewers. Sammy's family was in the crowd, including his son Michael, who was celebrating his second birthday. In the sixth inning Sammy faced pitcher Jason Bere. Whack! Sosa hit his 60th home run over the center field wall! He rounded the bases and was hugged by his teammates. When he reached the dugout he held up a sign that said, "I love you Dominican Republic."

After the game, the Brewers' manager said, "He's one of the game's real treasures. He's done something nobody before has done. Nobody has worked harder than Sammy to get where he is."

Sammy smacks his 60th home run of the season against the Milwaukee Brewers on September 18, 1999.

November 12, 1968	Sammy Sosa is born in San Pedro de Macoris, Dominican Republic.
June 16, 1989	Sammy plays in his first major-league game.
June 21, 1989	Sammy hits his first major-league home run.
July 29, 1989	Sammy is traded from the Texas Rangers to the Chicago White Sox.
March 30, 1992	Sammy is traded from the Chicago White Sox to the Chicago Cubs.
July 11, 1995	Sammy plays in his first All-Star game.
August 20, 1997	Sammy hits his 1,000th major-league hit.
July 7, 1998	Sammy plays in his second All-Star game.
August 5, 1998	Sammy hits his 250th career home run.
September 13, 1998	Sammy ties and passes Roger Maris's previous record of 61 home runs.
September 19, 1998	Sammy meets the family of Roger Maris.
October 21, 1998	Sammy receives the Roberto Clemente Award, baseball's highest honor for outstanding community service.
November 19, 1998	Sammy is named the National League's Most Valuable Player.
July 13, 1999	Sammy plays in his third All-Star game.
September 9, 1999	Sammy becomes the first player ever to hit 60 home runs in two consecutive seasons.
October, 1999	Sammy wins the National League Hank Aaron Award, which goes to the player with the most combined hits, homers, and runs batted in.

Sammy smiles to the crowd before the start of the season opener against the New York Mets on March 29, 2000.

GLOSSARY

academy (uh–KA–duh–mee)
An academy is a special school where people go to learn something. Sammy built a baseball academy in his native country, the Dominican Republic.

contract (KON–trakt)
A contract is the form an athlete signs when he or she agrees to play for a team. Sammy signed his first contract when he was 16.

drafted (DRAF–ted)
When athletes are drafted, they are picked to play on a professional team. Sammy Sosa was first drafted by the Texas Rangers.

Hall of Fame (HAWL uv FAYM)
A museum of the greatest athletes in any sport is called a Hall of Fame. Sammy wears number 21 to honor Roberto Clemente, who is in the Baseball Hall of Fame.

inning (IN–ning)
An inning is a part of a baseball game in which each team gets to bat until it gets three outs. Sammy once hit two home runs in the same inning.

major leagues (MAY–jer LEEGZ)
The best and most important baseball teams are in the major leagues. Sammy's team, the Chicago Cubs, is in the major leagues.

minor leagues (MY–ner LEEGZ)
The lower levels of professional baseball are called the minor leagues. Sammy started out in the minor leagues before working his way up to the major leagues.

third-world (THERD WERLD)
Small, underdeveloped, poor countries are called third-world countries. The Dominican Republic, where Sammy grew up, is a third-world country.

INDEX